Short Stay

A Poetry Collection By Cindy Collins

Internal illustrations by Cindy Collins.
Cover illustration by Talie Collins.
ISBN: 9798364351616

This poetry collection is named *Short Stay* because, simply put, that is what this book is. It is comparable to a short stay at a psychiatric hospital, where you are introduced to all different kinds of people and their disorders. This collection also serves as a short stay inside the minds of the mentally ill.

Please be aware that this poetry collection touches on triggering subjects such as mental illness, self-harm, sexual assault, and suicide. Topics such as self-harm and suicide should never be romanticized. The poems written in this collection are fictitious representations of the severely unwell. Read at your own discretion and remember to practice self-care and look after your mental health needs.

I dedicate this poetry collection to my beloved sisters Ayla, Talie, and Kristina. Thank you for supporting me during my short stay.

Short Stay

Short Stay is a poetry collection
Using rhyme and prose

With a mental illness theme
That shall inform and expose

Representing the truly fragmented
The melancholic and sad

Each poem is composed by a woman
Predominantly mad.

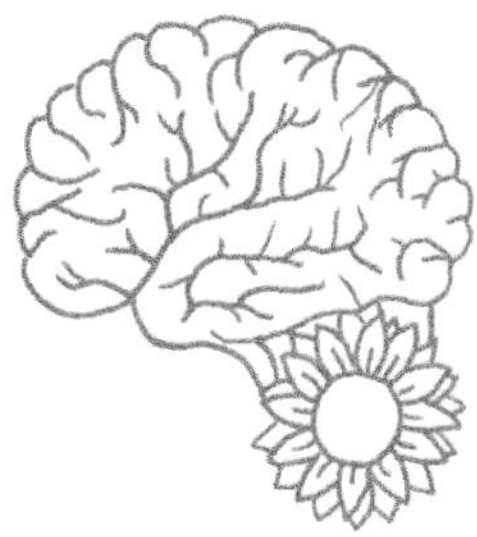

The Ward

Confined to these four walls
The piercing sound of silence

Psychiatrists and Seroquel
We pledge our compliance

Arduous and enervating
Describes each elapsing hour

But if we welcome treatment and assistance
Recovery is within our power.

Distractions

Mental illness
Shall never extinguish
The flame that has ignited inside

Regardless of the affliction
Exists a beautiful addiction
Erasing thoughts of suicide

For a simple delight
It is to write
If it provides your existence
With pleasure

And every scrawled phrase
Sets that fire ablaze
It is a joy you cannot measure.

Numbers And Letters

He was intelligent, overly perceptive
And his mathematical and literature
Examination scores were attestation
That he grasped difficult concepts

He was *the boy who knew everything*
Often seen with a blue ballpoint pen
Residing beside his expensive eyeglasses
And tucked gently behind his ears

He often hummed
Olden day show tunes to himself
As he read bulky historical textbooks
And his favourite pastime was
Studying intricate foreign languages
On the sunlit balcony in springtime

Numbers and letters were his ally,
It was his way of making sense of the world
If he was anxious, it was never revealed
If he was depressed, it was never communicated

His yearbook labelled him
Most Likely To Succeed
But intellect does not necessarily imply popularity
For perhaps he was far too clever for his own good

He viewed the world in black and white
Because though numbers and letters
Made unmitigated sense to him
Social interactions were incomprehensible
Regardless, his eccentricity was praised
By teachers, by his relatives and his co-workers
If only that would have sufficed

He was *the boy who knew everything*
I merely wish he had known his merit and value
Perhaps then,
He would not be tied down to a white gurney
With a large tube shoved down his throat

Numbers and letters were his medicine
But now antidepressants are

And the only numbers that can comfort him now
Are the ones written
On his unique identification band
Tied loosely around his left wrist.

By The Hour

I was once provided with helpful advice
I initially considered somewhat strange

That if you replace pessimism with positivity,
Your entire existence will surely change

For I have now discovered pure contentment
And I have grown audacious and strong

Because I no longer seek peace
And joy externally
I realised it has been within me all along

It is peculiar by far, and quite bizarre
That happiness was always in my power

My existence has altered,
My suffering has halted
I am recovering further by the hour.

The Child Is Gone

When we were young
Our wings carried us
Beyond the stone fortress
We called home

The years progressed
As did our maturity
And the kinship we cherished
Became a distant memory,
Fading without a souvenir

Now, gone are the days
Where we truly belonged.

At The End Of The Day

I rested against the lonely pine
With a poetry collection in my pale hands
And I contemplated my simple existence

Rainbow lorikeets and various other songbirds
Trilled a mellifluous melody from the treetops
And the morning sun shone
Through the narrow pine needles
Like a warm, gentle embrace

I placed my paperback companion
On the withered summer grass
And smiled blissfully towards the cloudless sky

Many a year has now elapsed
And in the end, I survived
Perhaps I surrendered
Components of myself along the way,
But I survived, nonetheless.

Visual Disturbances

Perceptible reality of the psychotic
May seem to be bizarre fiction to the majority

But my hallucinations are my visible truth
Because our observations are our actuality
Even when our senses, too, betray us.

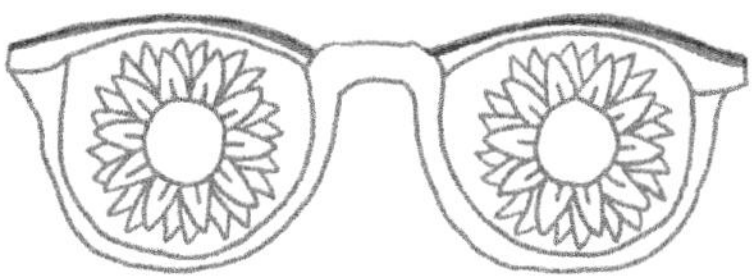

It Gets Better

On Sunday morning, I woke up, and I was happy
I sprang out of bed flooded with euphoria
And prepared a steaming cup of cappuccino
I sipped the appetizing coffee
Its delectability I had never appreciated
I went about my morning routines
My family greeted me with endearment
And I felt gratitude for their existence
There were no disputations this morning

I sauntered to my occupation promptly
Admiring the colourful environment
My surroundings were brimming with beauty
Why had I never noticed?
At my profession I was joyously welcomed
And tasks did not seem so tedious
I was simply radiant

Upon returning to my apartment
I concocted a nutritious meal
The scent of which was wondrous
The taste of which was enchanting
Before I slumbered, I expressed thanks
For the life I was assigned
And for all that has been provided
I had discovered that I could
Manifest my own happiness
As every day is a new dawn,
A blank slate, a tabula rasa
It is fact that suffering is never permanent

On Sunday morning I woke up happy
Or at least I would have,
If I had held on for just one more day.

Malfunctioning

Out of Order.
Parched, I craved
An affordable beverage

Except this vending machine
Is well-nigh as broken
As I am.

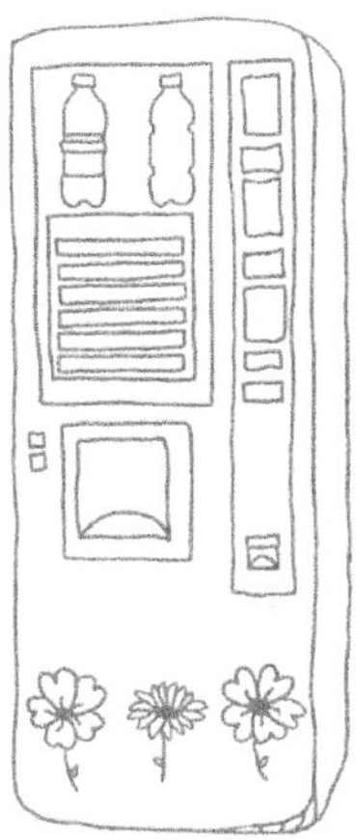

Starlight

I once surmised they were fireflies
These whispering stars
Multitudinous fireflies
Lingering in the ether

The radiant scintillating lights
Are faintly visible from my window
I contemplate their splendour
Momentarily intrigued by their beauty
And for a prolonged duration
I gaze admiringly

I conclude this will be
Another sleepless nightfall
Through heavy eyelids I behold
Evening's silhouette
I am taunted by muffled murmurs
And phantasms in the shadows

With a porcelain cup
Brimming with endless dusk
I sip,
And pray for respite and clarity
Struck by acute insomnia,
I peer out of my barred window once more
The sight of the stars mollifies me
And whether they are fireflies or
Something else wholly
They are real, unfeigned
And to have something so real
In a confused, fabricated environment
That is enough.

Broken

Suffering in ways
One could never envision

My mind is fragmented
Due to this melancholic condition

In a shattered mind I can hardly escape
I attempt to ameliorate my segments
With ribbon and tape.

Intrusive Thoughts

I arrived at the local train station
With a paper ticket clenched in my icy fist
Light rain drizzled onto the platform
And the dark, billowing clouds were ominous
In the night-time sombre sky

Jump, my thoughts interrupt
Jump in the path of the oncoming freight train
Or your mother will meet her demise
Trepidatious, I count to five.
1, 2, 3, 4, 5, All is safe.

A train approaches, and I board it
Taking an empty seat at the rear
I gaze through the condensation-soaked window
Tapping my anxious feet rhythmically

Slam your head, my thoughts interrupt,
Slam your head into the glass
Or something regrettable will happen
To your closest friends
Neurotic, I count to five.
1, 2, 3, 4, 5, All is safe.

I depart the train at my destination
Humming a nervous accompaniment
To the city's cacophonous atmosphere
Which is teeming with pedestrians
And young children travelling to school

Hurt that child, my thoughts interrupt
Hurt that small child or else
You will die an excruciating death
Exhausted, I count to five once more.

1, 2, 3, 4, 5, All is safe.

The day continues with a similar structure
As my intrusive thoughts are near ceaseless
An interminable, fatiguing repetition
Of unwanted, heartless inner thoughts
Only altruistically resolvable by
Numeric compulsions

And as the day meets its end, I am debilitated
Tomorrow will be a comparable battle
As will be any subsequent days
The certainty of such undetermined

Because I still fear that some day
I will be unable to count to five
In the required timeframe
Or I may listen to my thoughts
And carry out the violent actions

1, 2, 3, 4, 5, no one is ever truly safe.

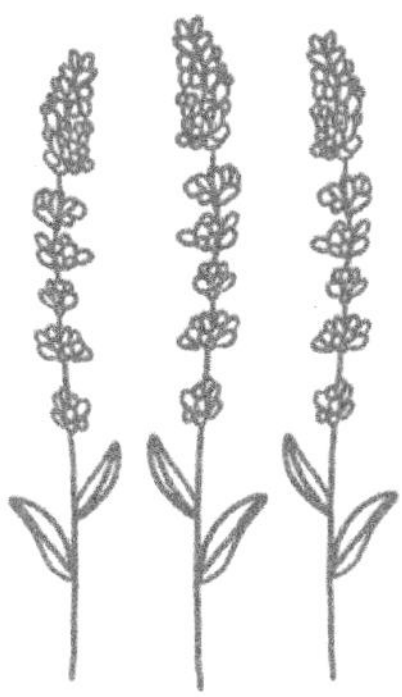

Fantasy

I am homesick for a destination
That simply does not exist

A place of tranquillity
Where we are loved,
Appreciated, understood

And within this mythical land
Our souls dwell
Our essences reside
Here we are unconfined

Promise me, my darling, someday
We shall travel there together
Even if only within
Our most beautiful daydreams
Even if it is only
Pretend.

Self-Aware

The lurking shadows emerge
Darkening like unlit vivid dreams

The toxicity of these visions
Confirm nought is as it seems

Suspending routines, pursuing the existent
I now perceive these observations
To be fictitious and inconsistent.

Individuality

When comparing yourself to society
The situation is bleak

For with constant imitation
You simply fail to be unique

Celebrate your individuality
Aspire only to heal and grow

You are deserving of contentment
As you are *much more important*
Than you might know.

Deteriorating

I am transforming
Into a living, breathing corpse

Dishevelled and disordered
Reality blurs and warps

Deterioration and destruction
Of personal hygiene

Functioning solely
On medication and caffeine.

Seasons

Rosie was the greenery in mid-spring
She was the winsome autumn leaves that
Would descend gently, and settle
On the damp pavement
She was the summer marigolds
And the frost-covered winter pines

Rosie was the embodiment of nature
And she deeply revered nature
She would set the earth ablaze
With her optimism and radiance
But in fire, foliage turns to ash
And hers are eternally concealed
In a rustic urn
Engraved with the haunting words
Now in God's care.

Rosie had appeared
Content in her existence,
A disturbing masquerade
But the world continues without her
And the seasons progress regardless
For she is merely another statistic
An additional soul irrecoverable
And Rosie, like so many others,
Will never again
Experience the tranquillity
And simplicity
Of things such as nature.

Melancholy

Spiralling deeply into madness
Perpetually intoxicated by sadness

A despondency within has now awoken
I am unfixable, desolate and entirely broken.

Choose Yourself More Often

Though you believe in destiny
And trust solely in fate

It may be time to embrace
That you are your own soulmate

You pursue love externally
Though it could be discovered within

If you did not love yourself previously
Today you ought to begin.

Maladaptive Daydreaming

A limitless compulsion
Actuality obscured
A lingering trance
Waking life disturbed

Blurred are the margins
Reality collapsing
Interfering with tasks
Fantasy encompassing

An overwhelming desire
To simply escape
To dissociate for hours
As daydreams take shape

Tis a laborious cycle
Triggering significant distress
Repeatedly and habitually
I suffer silently and obsess.

Love Never Dies

And before long, he was gone
Alongside the bulk of his suffering

But his pain never truly dissipated
It was only reassigned
To the individuals who will always love him
Those he left behind.

Silence

Selective mutism they categorised it
The way in some situations
I appear fully functional,
But in others I am reduced to silence
Why is appropriate eye contact compulsory?
Why, in certain circumstances,
Is speech obligatory?

I can recall instances where terror and anxiety
Halted my ability to speak- and I was reprimanded
Criticised for my quietude
Lectured for merely being overwhelmed
Unfamiliarity is discomforting,
I do believe silence can be a suitable response
But in silence, I forfeit my voice
And my capacity to communicate
In silence I squander my ability to say *no*

Selective mutism they classified it
But it is so much more than that,
It is a coping mechanism for perturbation
But you took advantage of my limitations
You exploited and abused my body
Selective mutism they labelled it
The way in some situations I appear fully functional
But when assaulted I am reduced to silence
Countless women have similar stories
And those capable must use their voices
Not just for themselves,
But for the copious who are
Imprisoned by their involuntary silence.

On The Corner Of Cobblestone Avenue

I approach the coffee shop
On the corner of cobblestone avenue
And the doorbell jingles feebly as I enter

I position my spacious satchel
On the wooden tabletop
And retrieve from it a lightweight laptop

The fragrance of ground coffee
Permeates through the café
The aroma of rich caramel espresso
Is appetising and entrancing

Thirsting for a dose of caffeine,
I politely order refreshments
And in the meantime,
I contemplate my enticing surroundings

The space is dimly lit by candlelight
An aged mahogany grandfathers
Clock ticks quietly,
In a relaxing and rhythmic manner
And the hum of mindless chatter
Creates a hospitable atmosphere

With the virescent linen napkin
I have been courteously provided,
I construct an origami butterfly,
As I am serenaded a contemporary melody
By the shop's antique record player

A cheerful barista advances expeditiously
With a timber serving dish in hand
I am presented with a golden-crusted scone

And a rich, steamy macchiato
I nibble on my delectable treat
And sample my liquid intelligence
The coffee engulfed in slight ripples

I switch on my high-end silver laptop
And commence my daily writing
Savouring the ambience,
Relishing in the moment
This is pure tranquillity.

Mood Disorder

Constantly fluctuating
Creating a violent inner feud
Aggravating, agitating
I cannot supress my mood

Emotions are oscillating
Like a precarious swing
Mania converts to depression
It is undetermined,
What my next episode shall bring.

Now Only A Concept

I wish you existed

I am no stranger to darkness,
But I despise that my life is a void
Without the light you might provide

I wish you existed

Insomnia keeps me awake
And sleep paralysis displays no malicious entity,
But your potential silhouette

I wish you existed

I mentioned the idea of you to my psychiatric team
They informed me that certain medications
Will quieten my fixation on the imaginary
Though, I do not want to relinquish you

I wish you existed

Because once, you did
And now you are merely a memory
Another ghostly shadow in my peripheral
Another whisper in my tortured head

I wish you still existed
Because I miss you
Unfathomably.

Health

In a beautiful country
With an abundance of wealth,
Why disregard our mental health?

Newer treatments and therapies
Are in dire need of discovery
If we are to have any hope at all
For mental health recovery.

Reclusive

Companionship is highly exhausting
I crave prolonged personal space

The freeing sensation of solitude
Is one that no interaction can replace

It is acceptable to favour being lonesome
As long as you use your solitude to heal

For solitude can be therapeutic
It has an intriguing appeal.

Lost

Disorientated in a world
I shall never comprehend
This is not an existence
I would candidly recommend

I have misplaced my mind,
My sanity has been neglected
I disregarded my antipsychotics
Now my rationality is affected.

Continuing On

In the shadow of an aged oak tree
And with fingers flecked with indelible ink
I scrawl in mere reminiscence
Of an altruistic departed soul

My writings are unintelligible and inarticulate
The pages are smeared with teardrops
And the notebook is overburdened
With scribbled annotations

I narrate his existence in continuance
The inscriptions describing a life ameliorated
A fulfilling life from beginning to end

But these words are fiction
For he did not endure
All that remains is his neglected journal
Left behind prior to his demise
And even if it is a fantasy,
He deserves a happy conclusion

As an accomplished wordsmith
I have the ability to provide a suitable ending
So, I shall narrate his unfinished story
And pretend he perseveres
Because, for now,
The alternative is far
Too excruciating
To accept.

Stay Positive

Do not despair for being disordered
Remain optimistic and keep moving forward

Your condition is merely a fleeting state
In time, you will surely recuperate.

Paying It Forward

Propagating positivity,
He is now enraptured
With his simple existence
He beams at traveling pedestrians
Complimenting strangers,
Spreading his exuberance

They say euphoria is contagious
It can liberate the broken
His well-being is a corroboration
That happiness and goodwill
Can be immensely healing
Now, his sole ambition
Is to be merrily attentive
He is adamant that every individual
Should feel recognised, acknowledged,

For he was once disregarded
And entirely overlooked
Almost prepared to abandon hope altogether
But kind-heartedness and benignity
Alleviated a sizeable fraction
Of his prolonged suffering

And although merely smiling
At citizens in the street
May not change the entire world,
If his goodwill could save
Just one life,
That would suffice.

Not Of This World

I was embraced by the galaxy
When all I desired was space

I now recognise that amongst the stars
Exists my birthplace

In my universal mind, nought is as it seems

I am dwelling between reality
And my most exuberant daydreams.

Schizophrenia

White walls murmur
Mental state- chaotic
Screaming from within
Paranoid and psychotic

Padded cells, electric jolts
Tis simply no vacation
Submerged in paranoia
Prescribed antipsychotic medication

Isolation, agitation,
A persecutory delusion
Hallucinations, illusions
Uttermost confusion

An exceedingly horrendous illness
Once you fall sick
Welcome to the harsh reality
Of the schizophrenic.

Keep Going

Inexorably growing stronger
Just persevere for a little longer

You may be residing in perpetual doom
But *I assure you*, my child,
You will promptly bloom.

Detoxified

I was never proficient at mathematics
But I do not struggle to enumerate the days

Since I announced I would remain sober
And halt such a toxic drunken phase

The depression has subsided
Once an alcohol-fuelled affliction

I am now abstinent and liberated
From the demons of addiction

The liquor cravings still transpire
The intrusive thoughts- unnerve

But I desire to be dependable
And become the clear-headed father
My children *truly* deserve.

Familiarity

Because I am accustomed to my suffering
I consistently choose hardships
Sometimes, somehow,
Familiarity is comforting

And it may be agonizingly unpleasant,
It may be another's most horrific nightmare
But I do not wish to wake,
Because I am accustomed to my suffering,
And the pain is *all I am*, and *all I know*.

Flight Risk

When emotions soar, as do I
Intrusive thoughts intensify

An inclination to dart beyond
A thrill it can be to simply abscond

And though it is freezing, and I am alone,
It is alluring- to explore the unknown

Hiding out of sight, incessantly concealed,
My next destination is yet to be revealed.

Nightmares

Reality and imagination
Blur together at the seams
Impossible to determine
Whether actuality or dreams

The confusion itself
Is semi-enlightening
It is peculiar that fiction
Can be *ever so frightening.*

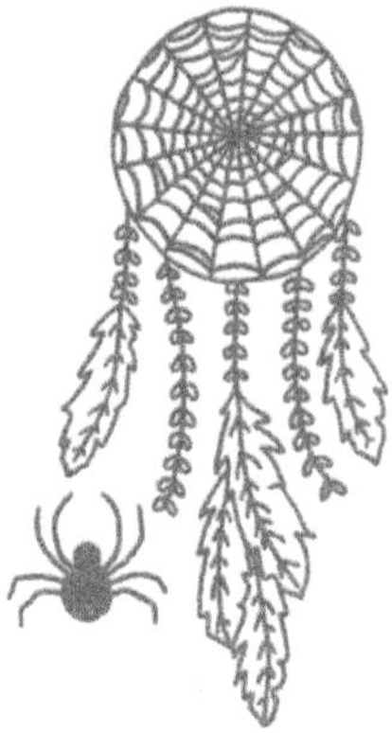

Asking For Help

Mental illness wreaks
A burdensome existence

Do not hesitate to seek
Guidance and assistance

Even if newly unwell
And you do not yet understand

You can convalesce and improve
With an amiable helping hand.

The Dressmaker

I would stitch together
Lengths of fabric
As though piecing together
The constituents of my life

But though I had a dressmaker's talent
I could not retract my blunders
And now, I just wish
I could sew my damn mouth shut.

I Can Save Her, Still

Whenever I consider suicide
I imagine not just eliminating myself
The individual I am currently, today,
But I envision ending the life
Of the sweet little girl
With white daisies in her golden hair
Who greeted the world with exuberance

The valorous little girl who relished
Descending down grassy slopes
On torn fragments of cardboard
And adored reading fantasy novels
On pearly white sand shores
The girl with inspiring potential
Who maintained that there was
Beauty in all of mankind,
And we must search for it ourselves

So, whenever I consider suicide
I remember that little girl
For she still exists, deep within
And I could never end the life
Of a human soul so inordinately kind
Remarkably free-spirited and innocent,
Because she deserves better,
She deserves to live,
And it is entirely up to me.
I can save her, still.

Isolation

Hyperventilating,
A vacant room of stone

Every second agitating
Perpetually alone

Inescapable solitude
Impossible to flee

Incarcerated by my unstable mood
Yearning to be free.

Art Therapy

Portraits on canvas
I smother mine with charcoal
Producing an impeccable depiction
Of my darkened psyche

Dust descends from my artwork
Showering the carpet with black powder,
Tarnishing a once immaculate classroom

Glimpsing briefly at the patient neighbouring me
I observe an effulgent sketch
Jovial, dazzling, cheerful and vivid
Very much dissimilar to my own

Disheartened, I attempt erasing my creation
Only to be left with a defiled, smudged canvas
And coal-stained fingertips

Tossing my artwork aside, exasperated,
I obtain a blank slate, acquire paint,
And produce an uplifting, exuberant picture
Complete with sapphire skies
And silver lining.

Street Kids

Teardrops on the pavement,
Her rucksack shabby and defaced

Limited possessions,
She roams the night with haste

The wintry chill exacerbates the desolation within
Famished, parched, and debilitated
Wounds and lesions cover her pale skin

Undetectable amongst the city crowd
Naught suspect the dire truth

She is homeless and psychotic
A runaway youth

Statistically, death is imminent
Or alternatively she will be jailed

This is another despairing example
Of how the mental health system
Has failed.

Grieving

Sinking deeply in disdain
Suffering with incalculable pain

Submerged in grief
Immersed in sorrow

No guarantee of awaking tomorrow.

Perseverance

Stargazing at cloudless twilight
The wind a gentle caress
Steamy hot cocoa warming my palms
As I relax against the fireplace

Devouring fragrant baked cookies
Crammed with crisp macadamias
And the drizzle of soft winter rain
As it pitter-patters against the tin canopy

The scent of fresh soil and foliage
Succeeding a flash tropical storm
The first vermillion tulip to blossom
Ensuing a misty sunrise

The embrace of a snuggly plush critter
On a frosty, wakeful night

And you.
These are the reasons I stay.

Dangerous Hearts

We were a cyclone of passion
Fierce, hazardous, wild,
And we were infatuated
With the mere concept of love
But our *love* was a silhouette
Of its true definition

We were not in love, we were in lust
And combined we were not soulmates

We were a cyclone of passion
Untamed, fiery, foolish
And we were infatuated
With the concept of a feeling
Of which we were incapable
Our *love* was dangerous,
Unwise, reckless, artificial,

And so, I knew straight from the start
Neither one of us would make it out alive.

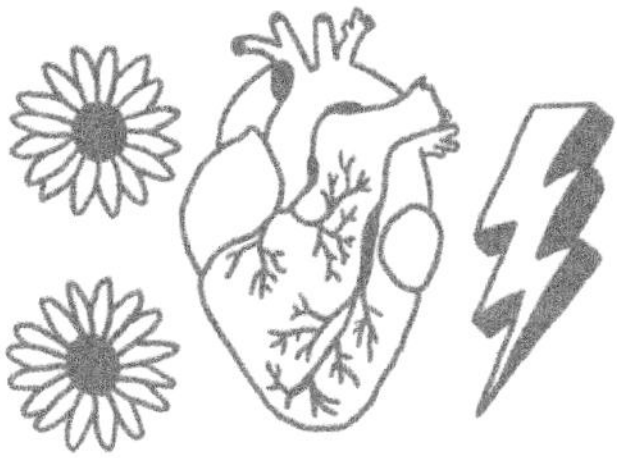

Fitting In

Her façade perseveres
Chameleonic disposition

Pretence and deception
Her sole ammunition

A personality fabricated
Unreservedly pretend

Imitating neuro-typicals
In pursuit of a friend.

Hallucinations

Illusions, auras, flickering,
Pattering in the ceiling
Silhouettes accompanying
This dreaded, sinister feeling

Skin-crawling sensations
Negative commands
Perceiving apparitions
Observing liquifying hands

Impossible to determine if merely imagination
As the whisperers' content varies
In this constant communication

Tactile, visual, auditory,
This nightmare is unfaltering
Horror and torment thrive,
Insanity ne'er altering

An array of antipsychotics
A vastly copious list
I long for some improvement
A plea for the capsules to assist

Perhaps I shall never escape
This persistent confusion
Even if my observations are purely
A delusion.

You Make Me Happy

Misty daybreaks and morning dew
The rising of a crescent moon
Duplicate rainbows in a sky of blue
Devouring ice cream with a wooden spoon

Harvesting fruit from springtime trees
Opening a brand-new pristine book
Picnics in a summer breeze
Lagoon fishing with a silver hook

Lengthy, warm lavender baths
Freshly baked walnut bread
Wandering through hilly woodland paths
Picking flowers coloured azure and red

All that these activities and moments do
Is bring me pure contentment and pleasure
But if I compare any one of these things to you
My dear, they *simply cannot measure.*

Shivers

My illness is a winter
Prolonged and icy cold
Improvement appears feasible
Then the chill returns ten-fold

My glacial mind is shattering
Into shards of wintry madness
I am submerged in the blizzard
Of my own perennial sadness.

Goodbye Letters

I battle the intrusive perpetually
But the wicked thoughts triumph
Suicide is liberating
They kindly assure me

I put quill to parchment
As teardrops blemish the ink
With multifarious phrases
I convey my *farewell*

This is the grand conclusion
To a pitiful existence
Destination- oblivion.

Where The Heart Is

Long ago,
We found immaculate sanctuary
Amongst the green speckled trees
Where the sun beamed radiantly
And petals unfurled delicately in the breeze

This haven we had discovered while young
Sung its own beauteous song
Wildlife greeted us harmoniously
Along the picturesque billabong

In time, we found again nature's refuge
A lifetime succeeding our youth
Our hide-away was desolate
Such is time's devastating truth

For the flowers no longer bloom
And the billabong is dry
Even the light summer breeze
Has ceased its melodious lullaby

But although our sanctuary is exanimate
And all its beauty has wasted away
Its allurement was my childhood
And in my heart will it eternally stay

For nothing is truly gone
If you keep its joyous memory alive
In our dreams, our haven endures
And within, our refuge will thrive.

Domestic Violence

Abuse is the black hue
Of romance dwindling

Serenity transitions to mayhem
Intimacy transforms to misery

Traumatic
Still, no absence of love
Precarious
Still, inviolable

A tortured heart perseveres
Unlike one unreservedly
Broken.

Detention Centre

Sanity as unattainable as
The sharp knives concealed
High upon the mantelpiece

Eleven, as of yesterday
Sinister childhood cogitations

Defined by conduct, arrested anew
His blunders will condemn him
Long after his juvenescence.

Lost Without You

Like plunging deep
Into a glacial river

Like the sensation of a
Plethora of knives
Perforating my flesh

Like plummeting
Rapidly from the ether

Internally, *this is what I endured*
When you departed
For the final time.

Falsities

My experiences may seem rather peculiar
To a rational outsider who cannot grasp
The concept of the inexplicable

But I assure you,
I experienced these memories nonetheless
And that is the saddest thing about insanity,

All of my stories are true
Regardless of if they ever really occurred.

Escorted Outings

In winter's shadow
We proceeded to the ocean on a rickety bus,
Teeming with patients and nurses

I sat in the outermost seat
Isolated in the presence of the fellow unhinged

Upon arrival, we tossed silver coins
And seashells into the ferocious waves
As the salty sea stung our open lacerations

The daybreak was lustreless
A tempestuous rainstorm imminent
Nevertheless, it was a taste of liberation
A flavour I would much prefer
To the unpalatable and traumatic
Corridors of the ward.

The Voices In My Head

There lurks a thriving nation
In the wilderness of my mind

They whisper in tongues
Compassionless and unkind.

Holding On

Remain positively optimistic
And keep all hope alive

For aspirations are healing
You may yet survive

Because an ounce of hope
Can kill mountains of pain

Strive to become a vivid rainbow
In a dark world abundant in rain.

Shattered

He observed his aircraft
Folded from tissue-paper
As it soared rapidly
Through the hospital's corridors

He once believed he too, could fly
A delusion, of course,
With excruciating repercussions

He recalls plummeting
And his knees kissing the pavement
These vivid evocations torment
His fragile mind incessantly

Now, he is permanently immobilised
From a temporary misbelief
Incapacitated as a regretful consequence

Medication may ameliorate his insanity
But no pills nor therapy can liberate him
From the wheelchair
He now depends on.

Busy Minds

Be watchful at dawn
Whilst you wake from sleep

This is the eerie hour
Where obsession shall creep.

A Break In The Clouds

Incessantly waiting for a break in the clouds
To assist in the growth of my garden
I water the sprouts with salty tears
As the sunrise turns crimson

They say beauty grows in misery
With pain these flowers shall bloom
Yet, though the foliage is abundant with agony

The branches collapse
The dry mire smothered with withered leaves
My petals crumble in the wind, and
Across the entire barren field
The now aureate sunlight carries my sorrow

The vast wasteland is my madness
But still, I anticipate a seedling of hope
For even on the darkest of days
When we hurt, we grow.

Joy

Simply choose happiness
Every once in a while

And never let a single soul
Dwindle your smile

Today is a new beginning
Evolve into your perfection

Promise that you shall never look back
You are not headed in that direction.

Silver Lining

I worry excessively
Regarding the future ahead

The voices manipulate my habits
I am misguided and misled

I tremble at the notion
That I shall never progress

To a brighter tomorrow
Far away from distress

Depleted by insomnia
Disquieted and forlorn

My entirety damaged
Soul fragmented and torn

This is my situation
As lamentable it may appear
Though with family and supports
I am grateful to be here.

Remorse

He had a smile that rivalled
The luminosity of the sun
Until the sombre colour
Of immense regret
Battled violently and won

Now, he is fragmented
Mere seconds from his death
He wishes he made amends
Before he drew his final breath.

In Your Hands

Take care of me
Not materialistically
Nor avariciously
But simply emotionally

Take care of my soul,
My fragmented heart,
My wellbeing,
For my life is in your hands.

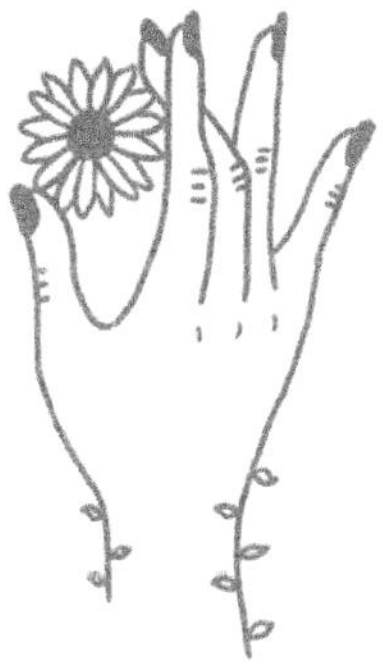

Self-Destruct

I spill my darkest secrets
To each stranger that crosses my path
I divulge every ounce of tumult
In a dazzling display of emotion

I want to frighten them all,
Unsettle these individuals
An infinite cycle of *stay away*

For I am insanity incarnate,
Undeserving of adoration,
Unworthy of compassion

I alienate myself,
For I would rather deliberately
Sabotage a relationship
Prior to its commencement
Than be hurt and disconsolate
Beyond restoration
Much, much later on.

Unstable Relationships

Teeming with the residue
Of men who encountered their doom

Perpetually in tenebrosity
Her heart is a crowded tomb.

Pseudologia Fantastica

Substantial deception
Unnecessary lies
Concealed by a mask
An unceasing disguise

The compulsive urge
Is purely psychological
Mendacious and dishonest
Obsessive and pathological

Regardless of the situation
Emerges eloquent fiction
Fabricating every phrase
Is an unpredictable addiction

The falsities in question
Are significantly excessive
Divulging notable fables
That seem overly impressive

No reasoning necessary,
Rationale or motivation
Exclusively based on impulse
Narcissism and temptation

Exaggeration expressed
With every breath
He will remain a liar until his death.

Relapse

The downpour of rain
Forces all into ruin
Despite our attempts
A storm is a-brewing

A monsoon, a typhoon,
A raging tempest
I desired sobriety
But yet again,
I regressed.

Yearning For More

Disconsolate with longing
I miss feeding the geese
Fragments of stale bread
At the murky pond beside my cottage

I miss rendezvous with family
By the water's edge
Observing the night-time sunsets

I miss lucidity, serenity, being wholly untroubled
Yet, such a reality, for now, appears unattainable

Time has debilitated my mind
The overlapping memories of pure ebullience
Have grown distorted

The care-free world I once knew
Is nothing but a shadow
Hidden, concealed,
Far beyond these hospital walls.

Medication

Pills, pills
Swallowing the bizarre

A metamorphosis
To whom we really are

Whether antipsychotic
Or antidepressant

The habit we encourage
Is truly incessant.

Healing

Sanity is a process
We are all works in progress

This is not the unequivocal end
With patience and therapy
You shall be on the mend.

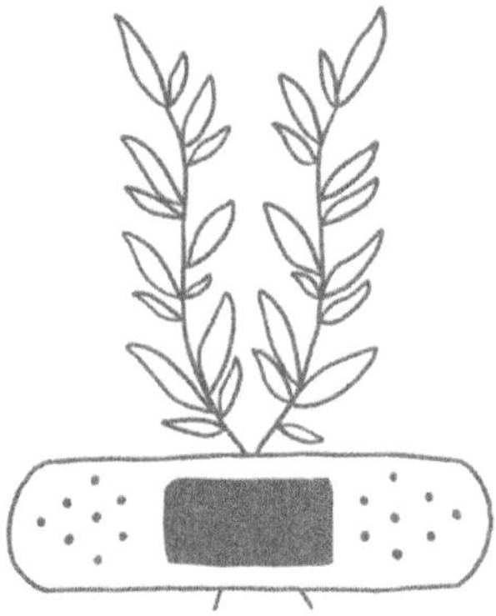

Mary-Anne's Supper

The clocks finally chimed midnight
Happy new year
Mary-Anne muttered vaguely
Whilst nibbling on a buttery pastry
Another repetitious year had concluded
In the uneventful sanatorium

Outside, a raging tempest
Catapulted shards of ice
Into the barred ward windows
Though, inside the bricked walls
The hospital was toasty and homely
Cups of steaming hot chocolate
Brought warmth to the kitchen-diner
For a fleeting moment, all seemed tranquil
Until splitting screams reverberated
In the corridors- a nightly ritual
The nocturnal cries and the whimpers
Had become Mary-Anne's lullaby
Once disconcerting, now almost soothing

She sipped her searing beverage
As a night-shift nurse approached
With two cerulean capsules
Somnolent, Mary-Anne guzzled
The remnants of her supper
Before retreating to her quarters
The passing months
Had become monotonous
The past irretrievable
The future yet uncertain.

Claustrophobia

Exceptional fear of crowded places
Perturbation in tiny spaces

I am terror-stricken, affrighted
Shivering with rage

Release me, I beg you
From this perpetual mind cage.

Broken Hearts

My love will remain
Though our hearts- contrasting

Some stories are not created
To be everlasting

Periodically romance
Diminishes with age

And time becomes nigh
To simply *close the page.*

ADHD

Repetition, fidgeting, hyperactivity
Absent-mindedness, impulsivity

Short attention span
Stability he is craving

Simply disordered,
Not just misbehaving.

Day Trips And Street Signs

The interior of the cramped vehicle
Carries the scent of stale cigarettes
An unwelcome, repellent odour

I gaze vacantly out the dark tinted windows
Muttering unintelligible secrets to the
Dusty, stained glass
As it whispers feebly in return

Scanning the boulevard,
I discern signposts and number plates
Forthwith, I am almost convinced
That they are indeed cryptographs
Puzzles that ought to be solved

I attempt to decipher the code
Like an operative on assignment
Yet, contemplating my recent diagnosis
I am partially ambivalent,

For I am either a prodigious detective
Alone in a world of the unenlightened
Or these beliefs are simply
A mere creation of my addled mind
And the concept of either
Is disconcerting.

The Healing Power Of Love

I hope you find someone
Who takes all of your broken, fragmented pieces

And gently stitches them back together
With the fragile, remaining strings
Of your splintered heart.

Bulimia

Overindulgence
A hollow-cheeked reflection

Binging then purging
War against imperfection

The pursuit of emptiness
Each day a blank slate

A perilous routine
For a reduction in weight

Regurgitating habitually
Death is brought nearer

Incessantly disappointed
With the body in the mirror

Dire repercussions
Stomach in ample pain

This is a dangerous lifestyle
For *anybody* to maintain.

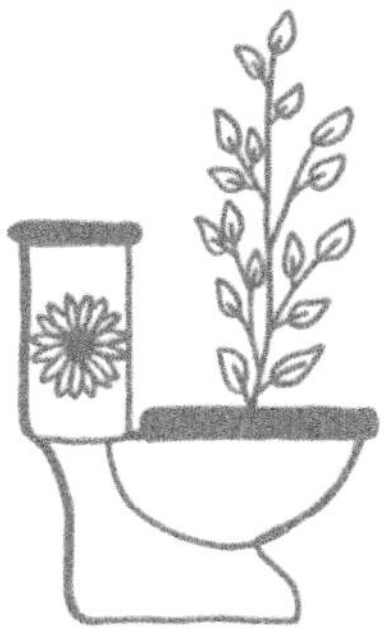

Demise

Lingering at heaven's gate
Not a single person noticed
Until it was much
Too late.

Unkind

Because the world is simply not kind

Because innumerable souls
Spend icy nights in the streets
Their sole possessions a soiled, grimy blanket
And a cardboard placard
Begging for loose change

And nations are held captive by war and terrorism-
Lives sacrificed daily by those
Obtaining their goals
With brutal violence and vindictive anger

Because disease and poverty impacts all,
Including the righteous and the innocent
Stealing lives, slaughtering children
It is barbaric how many perish
Before their life has even commenced

Racism, homicide, sexual assault,
Oppression, greed, inequality,
It breaks my heart,
Because the world is simply not kind
But you can always be,
Change is attainable,
And it begins with *you*.

Dawn

You told me it is never too late
To find joy in simplicity
I now encounter each day with this precept

For today, I awakened at sunrise
Performed my morning rituals,
And sauntered blithely to the suburb's
Dimly lit convenience store

I purchased a diet blackberry soda,
Formerly your favourite beverage
And smiled blissfully, reminiscing that time
You clumsily stumbled down the staircase
And your soda bottle shattered,
The liquid smothering the concrete

You were crestfallen about your wasted drink
So, I had offered you mine
These simple recollections comfort me
Years after their occurrence
Because if these soul-stirring memories
Remain inside my heart, so do you

After obtaining my blackberry soda
And returning my thoughts to the present day,
I traipsed down the boulevard
Remaining significantly optimistic
Despite the sombre forthcoming clouds

I danced along the daisy scattered hilltops
Dispersing dandelion seeds into the breeze
And when I approached a shallow lily pond
I skimmed flat stones
Across the murky water's surface

I inhaled the ambrosial scent of pine trees
As light droplets began to ascend
I twirled in the gentle rain

Then, almost instantaneously,
The drizzle turned to downpour
I frantically dashed to the shelter
Of the neighbouring bus stop
And once the clouds cleared once more
The morning sun had finally risen

You once informed me that
Each sunrise is an invitation to begin anew
That happiness is accepting
And embracing inevitable change

I was happy once, and I am happy once more
The choice had been mine all along.

Take Your Damn Pills

It is imprudent and irresponsible
To disregard your prescribed medication

You *cannot* improve your condition
With merely spirituality and meditation.

Self-Harm

Desperate for attention
Her world in debris

Suffocating, intrusive thoughts,
To a debilitating degree

Another cut, another scar
Torture to feel alive

It is much more than just a phase
Not all of us survive.

Wake Me Up

My worst nightmares once comprised
Of plummeting from mountain peaks
And sustaining life-long injuries

They contained my residence in a blaze
Or feeling trapped, claustrophobic,
In a compressing room

They involved failing mathematical examinations
And being pursued by faceless behemoths

These nightmares were haunting,
I could envisage no worse
But I learnt that these dreams were preferable

Because when I discovered you inanimate
On the bathroom floor
I realised that this,
This agonising scene before my eyes,
This was in fact
My *worst* nightmare.

Grateful

Welcome each morning
With a hint of gratitude

Be appreciative, optimistic
Have a positive attitude

Be confident and ambitious
Your heart will show you how

This is just a simple daily reminder
You are exactly where you need
To be right now.

Conflict

Anya is approaching her eighth birthday
I ceaselessly remind my younger sister
That she is brave beyond her years
She is too faultless to be a bystander
And the notion of such breaks my heart
I am fourteen in October,
But I am still brought to tears
By our parents' deafening altercations

My sister and I have secured ourselves
In our shared bedroom
Situated with our backs against the door
It'll be okay Anya consoles me
Teardrops trickle down my cheeks
And settle on the stained carpet
I take Anya's hand in mine
And force a melancholy smile
Which Anya returns innocently

Shouts from outside our barricade
Reverberate around the entire house
And my sister and I shudder
At the thumping thud
Of physical violence

I hold Anya in a tight embrace
Unquestionably,
We are beyond frightened
Our future is undetermined
But together, we feel loved
And *only* together,
We feel safe.

Behind The Romanticization

You state that I am indomitable
As I have seemingly endured
Every frenetic storm
Inspiration, you label me, for persevering
But I am not strong-minded, I assure you
You do not see the smudged black eyeliner
And pillowcases drenched with salty tears
You do not see the yellowing fingertips
From chain-smoking menthol cigarettes
Collected from the cement by the parking lot

You do not see the anger, the pain,
The drying blood sticking to cloth
Along my wrists and forearms
From a night-time dolorous
When sunrise itself was not definite
You do not see the toilet bowl
Flooded with the contents of my stomach
And the internal agony of swallowing
A variety of pills I located in the medicine cabinet
You do not see the ambulance lights
Flashing through the shattered window
Or the police officers
Restricting any desperate movement

I am not indomitable, I am dying
You do not see the unromanticized side
Of severe, debilitating depression
You will never see the true reality
Of such a horrific disease
Until it kills someone you love.

Fall

Can you sense the coldness in the wind?
Can you see that the flowers,
Too, are close to death?

The autumn leaves are cascading
Gently in the chilly breeze toward the damp soil
As the seasons lapse, inevitable changes
Force the falling leaves to metamorphose
From green, to yellow, to orange, to red
The flowers are wilting
Winter's death almost upon their petals

If summer approaches,
These woods shall be engulfed in flame
The foliage will burn and diminish
Long before the prospect of rebirth
They say it is an analogy of love
Swinging blithely from the cherry blossoms
By nought but a miniscule strand of vine

But then, too, you descend, swaying in silence,
Crashing recklessly into the damp earth
Heartbreak tears you into irreparable fragments
Green, yellow, orange, red,
Such beauty in passing
Will you, too, join the fallen?
Do you now sense the icy silence in the breeze?
Do you now see that all of the flowers are dead?

Thought Disorder

Tis a terrible thing, you will find
To be psychotic and doubt your mind

This disorder wreaks mountainous confusion
But persevere, I assure you
This malady shall not be your conclusion.

Anxiety

Overthinking is human
Until those thoughts turn to daggers
Suffocating in an open room
My lungs begin to shatter

Disoriented, nauseous, pure consternation
Feeling of impending doom without explanation

Mind in complete chaos,
My hands start to shake
Close to falling apart,
One more stressor and I shall
Break.

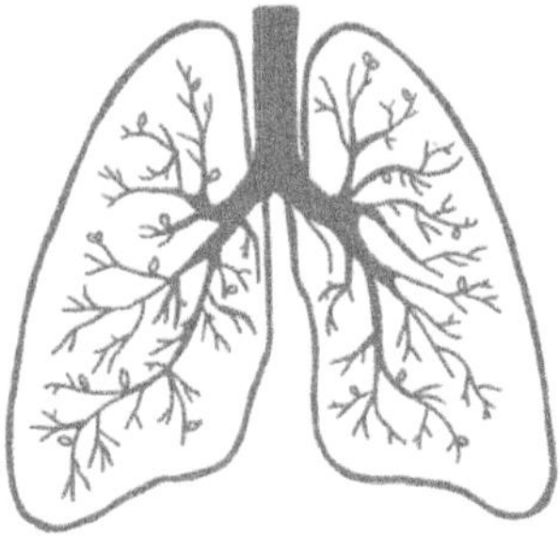

Inner Demons

Deserting the monsters
I shield deep inside

Of my destiny
I will solely decide.

Amnesia

I keep a white basket
Concealed under my hospital bed
Containing a multitude of keepsakes
Little mementos and souvenirs
In remembrance of a life unremembered
Grey post-it-notes are loosely attached
To each relic, describing their importance
When confused, or merely lonely,
I browse through my collection,
Reading the messy cursive ramblings
That explain each item's significance

A tiny round silver button
Is the smallest object in my basket
Its jottings reveal that it once embellished
An elegant, ethereal wedding dress
I can almost visualise its allure in my mind's eye
What became of my spouse?
A pair of large rose gold hoop earrings
Sit at the bottom of my receptacle
Allegedly they were a gift from my mother,
Worn proudly at my university graduation
Why has she not come to claim me?

Alongside these items is a circular pink seashell
Roughly the size of my palms
A pretty token from a childhood holiday
Where my younger sisters and I skipped rocks
Across the clear ocean water's edge
Where are my siblings now?
A rusty heart-shaped locket
Contains a photograph of an elderly couple
It once belonged to my grandmother
Why has she never visited?

A polaroid picture displays
My apparent friendship group
I do not recognise a soul
Have they, too, forsaken me?

The basket is teeming with objects,
A pinecone, a stuffed plush animal, a train ticket,
And it is evident that I lived a life well loved
I cannot recall much of my existence
But I do know
These are the worst months of my life
Not merely because I have forgotten
Those I loved
Those closest to me,

But because it seems that they,
Have all forgotten me too.

Goodnight

Night-time is my only solace
When I am comforted in my slumber

For when I am asleep,
I am truly without pain
When I am asleep,
I am nothing

And I would much rather a state of oblivion
Over the heart-rending agony
Of waking life.

Autism

I am not just a number, nor a statistic
The world is overwhelming, for the autistic

Crowds are bothersome and thunderous
Lights, blindingly bright
Some of us appear neurotypical
But alas, only at first sight

Every passing moment is brimming
With social expectation and distress
Let our silenced voices be heard
We are merely *different, not less.*

Comfort In The Known

I absconded mere minutes ago,
And my mind is congested with disorientation
Fresh air, I just require fresh air.
I keep sprinting, fleeing through the city
Where will I even go?

I glance at my surroundings,
Noticing the ombre skies
And the freshly poured concrete
I witness throngs of commuters
Going about their day
Are they even real? Is anything real?
How do I differentiate?

I arrive at the city gardens
And discontinue my hasty running,
Vanishing behind an overgrown oak tree
My heart palpitating,
My hands trembling,
I hyperventilate and collapse onto the damp soil
As vile voices echo simultaneously
In my busy, chaotic mind

I was confident that I was *special*
Chosen by deities to liberate
The entire earth from poverty,
I was certain I could initiate a revolution
With my exceptional knowledge and abilities
I thought I was having profound conversations
With intelligent alien life forms
This was my complete truth
Which I accepted wholeheartedly,
Imagine being informed that your
Entire reality is fabricated

That all you believe is a falsification
Earlier this morning, this was disclosed to me
Though I refuse to accept such a concept
Because who am I really
If my whole identity is based
On fantasy and delusions?

If my reality does not exist, then do I?
I am residing in a dreamland,
But if I am going to lose
Everything I am,
Everything I know,
Then I *do not want to wake.*

Beautiful Daydreams

I often observe a plethora
Of beautiful dreams
Behind my closed eyelids

My desires pervade my inner mind
Like a constellation of ambition
One day, I aspire to open my eyes

And be happy and content
With what I perceive and experience
In this actual, tangible world too.

Ignorance

Not at all a light switch,
Mental illness is a glitch.

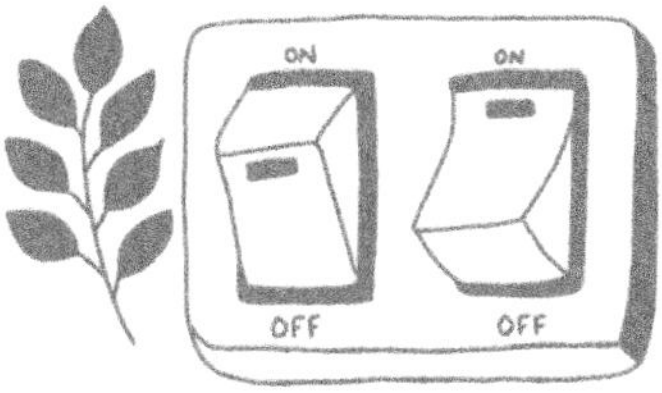

Egotism

You captivated me with an inferno of passion
Your red flags were magnetic
Enchanting my insecurities
Seducing my fragility

I remained benevolent through your cruelty
I continued to believe that you
Had a fragment of compassion
Deep within your shadow of a heart

I now understand exhaustively
You never truly desired me
For you are the embodiment of narcissism

The only creature you have ever loved
To any degree
Is yourself.

Tiny

You are a beautiful creature
Tormented by lies

And life is far too fleeting
To fret over size

Starving incessantly
To end self-hate

You are exquisite and worthy
Regardless of your weight.

Corridors

These hoary halls have promptly
Become my temporary home,

Where psychiatrists scrutinise
And the fragmented ones roam.

Confusion

My mind is addled
Begging to be cured

Upside down, dim
Unclear, obscured

I am wholly unbalanced
Abundantly concerned

Everything is incorrect
Reversed and overturned.

My Life Begins Now

I want to live.
I crave warm summer nights, stargazing
And philosophizing about the little, insignificant
Things that bring us immense joy
I crave heartfelt laughter whilst eating
Apple crumble as a close-knit family,
And climbing into bed
With warm sheets fresh out of the dryer

I just want to live.
I desire long walks,
Barefoot through national parks
And singing in the rain
As the droplets begin to descend
From an ombre sky
I desire bubble baths scented with essential oils
And hearing a captivating new song on the radio
As I drive leisurely through the countryside

I want to live.
I yearn for homemade baked goods
And roasting peanut butter smores
On a makeshift firepit in the garden
I long for the ability to appreciate
All the beauty in this world
To wake up eternally grateful
And to find the meaning in existence

I want to live.
I never wanted to die, not really,
I just wanted the pain to stop
The finality of ending it all
Was not a lasting intention
And now,

I am lying awake in a white hospital bed,
Somehow gifted with a second chance,
And I am beyond thankful

Oh, God, *I really do want to live.*

And I will take this opportunity now
To simply *start living.*

Impulsive Behaviour

Relapsing once more
I cannot halt this feeling

Instead of misdemeanour
I should spend more time
Healing.

Stay Kind

In a society so rapidly selecting hate
Strive to never discriminate

Leave discourtesy and incivility behind
Attempt to forevermore
Remain compassionate and kind.

Depression

The numbness is comparable
To a mind-altering pill
Everything is nonsensical
Yet time is standing still

Exceedingly exhausted
Difficult to comprehend
Then the aching turns to agony
I beg for it to end

Immeasurable sadness
The suffocation is inhumane
Every day repeats itself
Thousands of hours of pure pain

Written are far too many notes
Declaring my goodbye
And if my depression kills me tonight
I will be *more than ready* to die.

Borderline Personality Disorder

Vodka, scars,
A knotted rope necklace
Impulsive behaviour,
Promiscuous, reckless

Attention cries
Uncertainty ahead
A strong desire to die
But deep inside,
She is already dead.

Beauty

I am a rose garden
Rising from the earth

Every blooming flower
Accentuates my worth

Rainbows, tranquillity,
And bright sunbeams
I am continuing to grow and blossom
Creating the life of my dreams.

Uneasy

Restless as a mound of leaves
Trembling in the autumn breeze.

Please Do Not Turn Out Like Me

I pray that you never
Shed tears in a grimy lavatory stall
Press a blade to your flawless skin
Or starve until emaciated

I pray that you never
Become timorous or withdrawn
Abuse deleterious substances
Or lose hope and motivation entirely

I desire to be your role model
An exemplar, a positive influence
Though I lived a destructive lifestyle
I pray that you flourish,

Grow content and courageous
My dear child,
I have raised you the way I was not
Thence I pray, I plead,
With every ounce of my being

That your life will on no account
Resemble mine.

My Phantom Friends

The nightly shadows wail
As blaring as a locomotive

They are formidable
But companions, nonetheless.

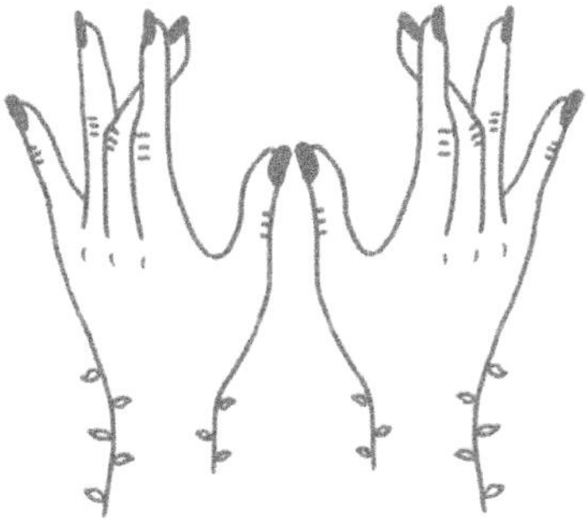

Escapee

Traipsing along the caliginous boulevard
A runagate minor- unbridled,
Unbalanced,
With formidable intentions,

She evades paramedics
And law enforcement authorities
Skulking between alleyways
Lurking in the dusk

She has escaped the institution
For the final time.

Child Abuse

Bless the young soul,
Tragedy raised

Bruises and tears,
Years enslaved.

Share Your Journey

Recuperation takes time
From a patient's point of view

In the meantime, recognise your worth
And ensure others do too.

Family Visitation

I apologise earnestly
For my shortage of appreciation

I was enervated, restrained in secure bindings
Too wearied and unresponsive
Due to medication and psychosis

Fear not, I am progressing steadily
And upon your return
I will express my gratitude
For your unremitting support
And love- *much reciprocated.*

Non-Compos Mentis

We abandon our sanity
Discard it far behind

We shall never be liberated
From our shattered minds

Caged and secluded
I repudiate my brain

For it is the sole reason
I am clinically insane.

Contraband

'Twas pearlescent daybreak
In the diminutive courtyard
With perturbation,
We lit a stale cigarette
Concealed marginally by dense foliage
The scent of thick smoke
And smouldering embers
Permeated the forenoon air
And a parade of ash
Waltzed past the barred windows

Lungs gasping,
We embraced the intoxicating thrill
Or disregarding the regulations
Of our psychiatric cage
We were addicted to
The euphoria of disobedience
As the sunlight grew crimson,
We extinguished the residue
Of the solitary cigarette
Vacated the confined courtyard
And dispersed
Benumbed,
From the modicum
Of insubordination.

Try Again

Pursuing stability
With limited success

Failure is a tedious part
Of the process

Persist, fight, battle
Do not surrender nor fear

You will recover, I assure you
If you simply *persevere.*

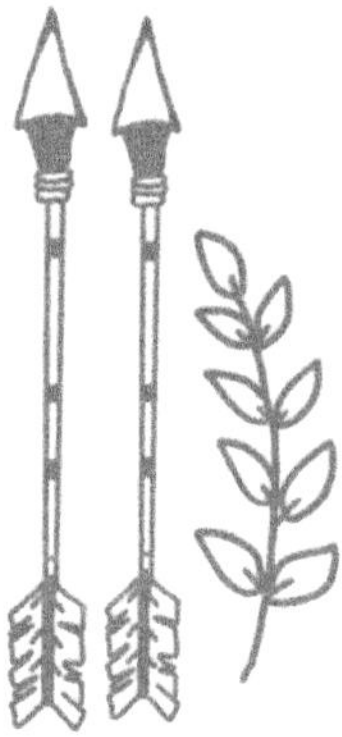

Dysmorphia

I do not pursue beauty,
But merely acceptance

I aspire to peer into the mirror someday
And not see my body as a burden.

Bipolar

In a cycle of depression
I am melancholic, forlorn
Constant isolation,
A duration withdrawn

It shifts to euphoria
I am promptly ecstatic
Considerably erratic, hyper manic

Slave to emotions
Pills bring stability
With the correct dose
Future of tranquillity

Now, a life in chaos
No apparent order
I have been diagnosed
With bipolar disorder.

Work In Progress

Remarkable to behold
Though yet to be perfected

Some souls are too radiant
To be merely neglected.

A Wise Trade-Off

Weary, indisposed,
I pull the linen duvet
Over my fevered cranium
A reaction to the cocktail
That promptly promised sanity

Side effects, though overwhelming
Are an imperative exchange
For, a temporary ailment
Is preferable
To unwavering psychosis.

Anger

Suffering in silence,
Resorting to violence

Severe exasperation,
Noncompliance.

The Monster Within

It is imperative that we impede
Our psychological demons

For only confrontation can annihilate
That potent fragment
Of our psyche.

Dark Obsession

Inordinately dangerous,
Remarkably intriguing

His mendacity is compelling
Captivating my attentiveness

I am enraptured, mesmerised, infatuated
Yet, regrettably,

Doomed.

Delusions

Over-suspicious, terrified
Fearful and insecure

Desperate for my carer
To soothe and reassure.

Homesick Alien

I have been transported
Into an inescapable foreign realm
This domain is unfamiliar, austere
They refer to it as an *asylum*

I am surrounded by monotonous brickwork
The atmosphere is unstimulating
And the inhabitants themselves
Are anomalous, outlandish, disturbed

Liberate me from this aberrant location
I assure you I do not belong
Authorise me to depart this world-
Return to my kindred and homeland

Where I know solace, security, love
And *all makes perfect sense.*

Alcoholic

A vodka-filled stomach
Fear trickling in my palms

A ramshackle heart
Extinguished cigars
Alcohol was bottled
My emotions, sadly too

Cheers to my demise
This time I shall follow through.

Emotional Instability

Emotions fierce opponents
Two combatant extremes

Like a tournament of chess
This is a ceaseless conflict.

Seclusion

Anguish accompanies
Each moment spent alone

But, regretfully, solitude
Is a vital stepping stone.

Anorexia

I am grotesque, wasting away
In the pursuit of beauty

And of my health the doctors vow
That my restoration is their duty

Fighting body dysmorphia
Pale as a porcelain doll

Consuming only oxygen,
The illness takes its toll

Another inch lost
It is weightlessness I crave

This habit of starvation
Will soon lead me to my grave.

Scars

Ripples in his skin
A disfigured regret

From a traumatic time
He would preferably forget.

Suicidal Ideation

Take me away, I can no longer remain
In a world that does not forgive

Lacking humanity, driven to insanity
I have lost my will to live.

Silence

An attempt to scream
Yet no words escape

My lips are forced shut
With stitches and tape.

Frozen With Fear

Submerged in icy thought, engulfed in fear
A beast emerges from the gelid deep
The creature is psychosis,
With a rimy grimace of torment
It taunts me with its hurricane eyes
As mine weep crystals of clear glass

I find fleeting sanctuary in the mist
But akin to my sanity, that too shall fade
I am imprisoned by two concepts
This embodiment of madness
And the glacial valley of my mind
Where the icicle shards of my strength
Are splintering, fragmenting like glass

I can find no deliverance,
For my mind and the beast are one
I am tentative, desirous to thaw my symptoms
Though, during the attempt
I may stumble over my infirmity
And in lieu of recovery
I may downright
Shatter.

Façade

Expressionless gaze
A contagious smile

This pretence will linger
For she is versatile.

Worthy

You are unique
No attribute ignored

Understand, dear child
What is real, is flawed.

Never Forgotten

You still visit me on despondent nights
When my sanity betrays me

I cannot decide which is more disconcerting
The fact that you have departed

Or that now you are nothing more than
A memory-fuelled
Hallucination.

Madness Theme Song

I sing a despondent symphony
A once euphoric melody
As constant as my heartbeat
The most emotional of arts

Beautifully melancholic
The instruments reflect my abnormality
Chords echoing through the ambience
The rhythm of an outcast

The harmony is compelling, yet
Darkening expeditiously
The acoustics are overwhelming
Music disconsolate
Silence unattainable

The doleful harmony is exacerbating
These tones will asphyxiate me
A frayed rope constricts my throat
I will no longer sing this broken song.

Anticipating The End

Inevitable is the caress of death
Its darkness forthcoming

Inching closer as the seasons progress
The concept of such is numbing.

Auditory

We shall never be silenced
For we are the voices inside
Ridiculing and minacious
We will coerce suicide

Heed our caution, we insist
Pathetic, pitiable soul
We exist to direct you
To accompany and control

These are perilous times
We have apprised you thrice
Obey our whispers without delay

Or we shall bring forth
Your demise.

Antisocial Personality Disorder

Monster, they cry
Inhuman, they dread

Calculative and cunning
His innocence is dead

Manipulative and scheming
No tenderness within

Loathing and fierce anger
Captivated by sin

Intrigued by adrenaline
Overpowered with wrath

Dark and spine-chilling
Is the sociopath.

Acceptance

An eternity alone,
Perpetually rejected

All I *truly* desired
Was to be wholly accepted.

Nymphomania

Compulsive, impulsive
Licentious, promiscuous

She is dependent on conduct
Perilous and reckless.

Hope

Even in the darkest of circumstances
Faith should remain

For recovery is feasible
You are only temporarily insane.

Dementia

Alice's son brings her daisies
Indistinguishable from the flowers
That blossomed in her garden
Countless years prior
Can she still recall their allure?

She has transformed into a woman
With mist and shadows behind her azure eyes
Without her son's habitual visits
She would be forsaken
Is that what she deserves?

Photographs have transmuted
Into vague strangers
These figures have vanished from her memory
And she has escaped theirs
She has lived a spiteful existence
Does her disease exonerate her?

Exiled from her own mind
And clinging to fragile hope
Her thoughts abandon her,
Withering like aged daisies
Though her son is attempting to forgive
Soon, *even he will be forgotten.*

Writing Your Heartbeat

You are evidence that existences vary
Yours was once brimming with
Uncertainty, instability, and strife

At times I write about you in my poetry
Simply to bring you back to life.

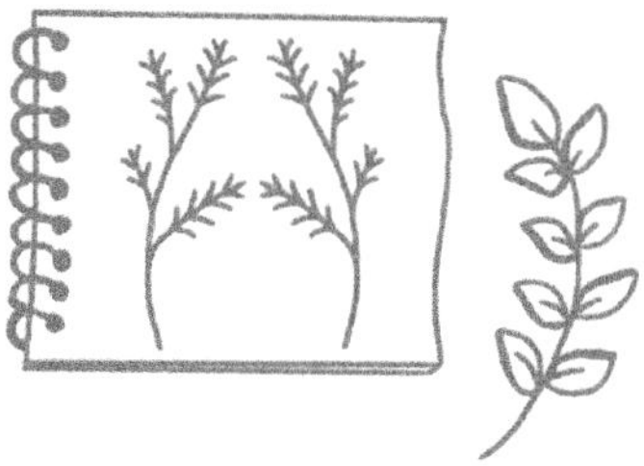

Mania

Intense energy
Intrusive thoughts, a sense of agitation
Psychotic symptoms added to the equation
Is a deadly combination

Injudicious behaviour, insomnia
In need of assistance
This mental illness brings
An immensely dangerous
Existence.

Cold Turkey

Desensitized, paralysed
Numbing withdrawals

My emotions are barricaded
Obstructed by walls.

Danger

The moon above was the only source
Of light in the tenebrous alleyway
Rachel crouched in the outmost corner
Uncorking a bottle of cheap alcohol

Her hands shook
As she raised the flagon to her chapped lips
Tears trickled down her cheeks
And settled on the dusty concrete,
As she traced her magenta bruises
With her index finger-
Souvenirs from a wrathful relative

She drank her entire beverage
Hoping to find guidance
At the bottom of the bottle
But as she consumed the last several droplets
No new counsel transpired

I just wish I could stay hidden here forever
Rachel muttered to herself
For dusky city alleyways may be perilous
But so is the concept of returning
To an abusive home.

I Shall Never Forgive Myself

I am not proud of my scars
As they are not battle wounds
They do not indicate that I was strong
Or brave, or some form of warrior

They are an unappealing reminder
Of an abhorrent phase in my life
A chapter I desperately hope to forget

I am not proud of my scars
And why should I be?
If I was truly brave,
I would not have harmed myself
In the first place.

Narcissistic Personality Disorder

Disregard of emotion
Uncurbed need for admiration

Sense of entitlement
Eminently hostile reputation

Inability to handle criticism
Inflated self-esteem

Exploiting without guilt
Compulsion to demean

A dangerous personality
Fuelled by narcissism and lust

This is an individual that
You would be unwise to trust.

Apparitions

In my peripheral
For an expeditious second

I perceive humanoid shadows
They leer and they beckon

At twilight they emerge
Petrifying and daunting

Their silhouette and mahogany eyes
Are exceptionally haunting.

Reckless

Caffeine and cigarettes
Experiencing life
Without regrets

Hazardous as it may appear
I accept that my future
Remains unclear.

Special

Perched on the auburn leather sofa
In the crowded sitting room
With a searing hot cocoa in hand
I scrutinise my fellow patients
With more than mere suspicions
Gyrating in my mind
I am gifted with other-worldly abilities
And because of such,
I can hear the clangs of machinery
Within all of the patients' flesh vessels
And the sounds of their gears and cogwheels
Of their robotic organs
Reverberating around the room
The ticking is ceaseless,
The mechanical echo, taunting
I have unearthed an abstruse secret
One that may effectuate great ramifications
If my brilliant abilities are detected

Disquieted, I sip from my scalding cocoa
Observing the non-human imposters
As schemes permeate my thoughts
I must act swiftly this time
If I am to prove their true identities
It is almost time for my
Forced nightly medication,
And my remarkable abilities
Will invariably deplete
Mere minutes after I swallow those toxic tablets
And until the effects diminish once again
I will no longer be gifted
I will no longer be...
Special.

Todd's Syndrome

A peculiar condition
Altering your perception

Curious and bizarre
Is it merely a deception?

Disorientation, distortion
Of vision, time, and sound

Micropsia, Macropsia
The symptoms will astound

It may influence your senses
Though it is not a hallucination

This condition, simply put
Is a bewildering complication.

Vanish

I wish to disintegrate
Like trifling grains of sand

This world is far too complicated
To completely understand.

Obsessive Compulsive Disorder

Compulsive behaviour,
Anxiety, repetition
A recurrent torment
Of subtraction and addition

Seemingly meaningless
The rituals may be
Only lengthy treatment
Can set me free.

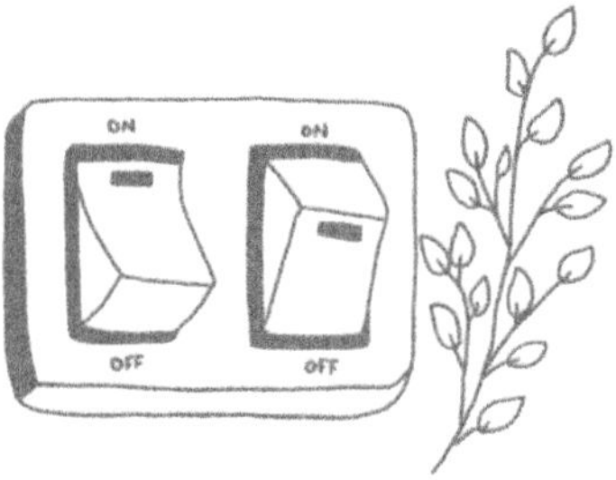

Unborn

Several months have elapsed
And your absence is heart-rending
My fingertips still quiver
As I sip my morning cappuccino
My voice still quakes
When I attempt to explain my chasmic loss
To those who will never truly understand

I planted a garden in your memory
Blossoming with hydrangeas
It is enchanting,
Comparable to how beautiful
You would have been

As I traipse by the flowers,
I envision you in my arms
Fast asleep, untroubled, safe,
Loved unconditionally

I never had the privilege of knowing you
But I glimpse your beauty in the stars
Alongside the other unborn angels
That departed the earth too soon

Wait in the skies patiently for me, darling
I will never forget you
And I eagerly anticipate the day
We *finally* meet.

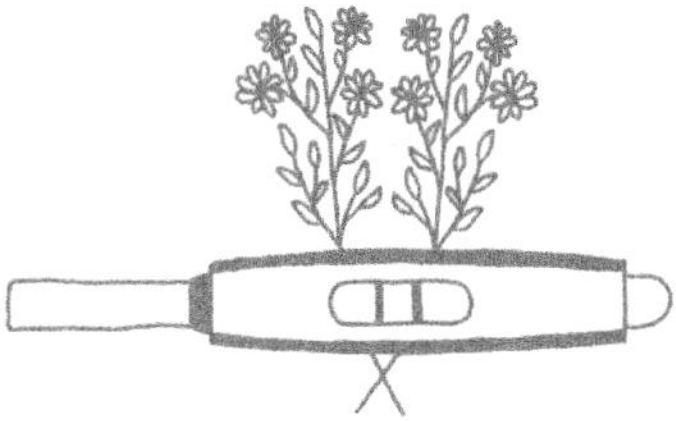

Better Days

Summer exuberance
The seaside salt in our hair

Paradise and sunbeams
Recuperation is in the air

I have learnt that life, unfortunately
Is not all happiness, peaches, and cream

But a high percentage of it *actually* is
Much more than it may seem.

Schizo-Affective Disorder

Alone,
I am in a crowded mind
A mood disorder and psychosis combined

Double the torment and the fear
This sinister disorder can be especially severe

Mania, hallucinations, delusions, sorrow
Persevering daily for a tolerable tomorrow

Treatment is interminable and symptoms persist
For the schizo-affective
No cure currently exists.

Red Flags

Standing alone is healthier
Than standing beside an individual

Who only utters the language
Of toxicity and abuse.

I Am My Past

Mistakes, regrets
They are simply not the same

For if I reversed time
And took back my supposed blunders

I would erase the entirety of myself
In the tedious process.

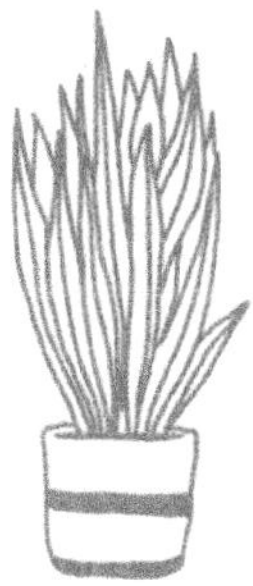

Behind The Diagnosis

My favourite colour is cerulean
My middle name is Grace
I fancy mountain hiking and bushwalks
On warm days when the sun shines bright
Through the dry summer leaves
Producing a picturesque kaleidoscope
Of radiance on the damp forest floor
I watch online documentaries regarding nature
I mostly admire
The programmes on honey badgers
They live a simple, happy life-
An existence I desire

I adore gardening with my younger siblings
Especially when they pick and bestow upon me
Yellow daffodils in bloom
I keep them in a vase on the mantlepiece
Until they wither and lose their beauteous petals
Even then I dislike discarding them
My euphoria grows with camping by the ocean
When the waves crash rapidly
Against the rugged, rocky cliffside
The sound echoing through the campsite at night
And I enjoy roasting pink marshmallows
On an open firepit as embers
Float gently in the wind

Alongside a support group, in the wilderness
I began meditative yoga
The clearing provides an adequate location
And this form of simple mindfulness is soothing
I am an avid adventurer
I travel with close relatives on a monthly basis
Exploring the outdoors, climbing oak trees

And venturing through the countryside
I take each day as an opportunity
To create more exhilarating memories
I now own a photography blogsite
And snapshots of wildlife and the environment
Crowd my silver digital camera
I flaunt my photographs to my family
During Christmas and Easter celebrations
As we share joyful stories
Of our combined yearly experiences

I attempt to make every nanosecond count
Because life is remarkably short
I try to remain optimistic
For I am courageous and adventurous
Independent, driven
I am ambitious
I am loyal and trustworthy
But most importantly, I am human
And though at times I still struggle,

This is who I am
I may have borderline personality disorder
But I will never let it define me.

Euphoria

Be radically happy for others
And your personal joy shall follow

Today's shared jubilation
Will bring a truly radiant tomorrow.

Munchausen Syndrome

Medical history inconsistent
Seeking commiseration and attention

Symptoms deliberately constructed
Duplicitous, illusive intention

A factitious disorder
Incessantly feigning disease

For tenderness and sympathy
She fabricates with ease.

Cycles

Flashes of a firestorm
Beneath my eyelids

The spark will reignite
In due course.

Home

My home is not a destination,
But a person where my heart resides

My soul will always be sheltered from storms
For as long as you protect it
In your homely hands.

To Belong

I carved empty words into my flawless skin
Because I noticed that the sought-after young girls
In my classroom had faded silver scars
Scattered across their wrists like constellations
I chain-smoked an entire carton
Of French cigarettes
Because I observed the trendy adolescents
During recess break sparking copious of their own
With their safety matches and vintage lighters

I imbibed two flasks of straight vodka
And consumed a handful of illicit capsules
On a desperate Friday night
Because I witnessed the popular students
Achieving exactly the same

I struggled desperately to be accepted
I craved negative attention,
Deeply desiring to belong
But liquor and happy pills did not satisfy me
For, regardless, I was not happy,
And this detrimental attempt
To be modish dismantled me

I forfeited my individuality, my identity
I unreservedly forgot who I was
All I wanted was to finally be noticed
I suppose my wish was granted
Disregarded in life,
Popular in death
It is heartbreaking how these
Things work.

Strength

With a spark of brilliance
She rediscovered her resilience.

Natural Disaster

The gusting, blustering winds of change
Quaked the earth in my slumber
I stood beneath the open doorframe
Rubble and debris collapsing in my vicinity

The booms of heartbreak reverberated
No escape imminent, no escape attainable
We were suppressing an impending apocalypse
And we were infinitely a doomed catastrophe

Nought could survive when we were together
Not love, and certainly not happiness
For you were a raging tornado
And I was a volcanic eruption afire

It was only *natural*
That we would be a *disaster.*

Ashes

Your grey, sooty cigarette smog has seeped
Its way into the upholstery
Of your favourite lounge chair
Which is now scorched
With cinders and burnt-out embers

Your lungs were once set alight with dusty flame
The glass smoke receptacle upon the fireplace
Is teeming with ifs and butts
Such a dangerous addiction,
And principally prolonged suicide

And the atmosphere
Of your antecedent living quarters
Is permanently befouled and polluted,
The air is death itself

I wish I could take your yellow-stained hands
And lead you far away from this distasteful,
Abhorrent compulsion
But alas, it is far too late

As your hands are already in ashes.

The Blues

You were blue, irrevocably blue,
Deep shades of sapphire and azure
But additionally morose, and dismal

You were cerulean
Beautiful shades of navy
And the deepest hue of aquamarine
Encapsulated by sadness and desolation

You were blue, eternally blue,
Then you were simply gone,
But since your untimely demise
I pay much more attention

To the spectrum of blues
In the morning skies.

My Sweet Addiction

I love and cherish you, immensely
As I love and cherish liquor

The compelling temptation
That causes light and sound to flicker

When disconsolate and melancholy
The compulsion consumes my soul

Intoxicated in madness,
The concept devours my essence whole

Your love and hard liquid refreshments
Are comparatively the same

When I lose all of my inhibitions
Both of such are to blame

I drink alcohol compulsively,
An addiction and a perilous tendency

But I would much rather be drunk
On your unconditional love
It is my true, honest dependency.

On The Mend

I have learnt to love myself
And be much more forgiving

Although alive,
I was not truly living.

Homebound

In my involuntary psychiatric admission
I have suffered, endured pure desolation

I have been strapped to a gurney, immobilised,
Whilst being injected with various sedatives

I frequented white-bricked isolation rooms
With small apertures on the doors
For bland, insipid meals to be passed through

I have been restrained against my will
Assaulted by unbalanced patients
Neglected by unsympathetic staff

Next time,
In lieu of another hospital admission,
I shall simply re-read this poetry collection
For it is far less traumatising
Than the nightmarish ward itself

My discharge papers have been signed-
I am homebound,
And though at this moment in time
I may not be thoroughly recovered,
And I may not be at all untroubled,
Or even happy within myself,

At least I now know
I just might live to see that day.

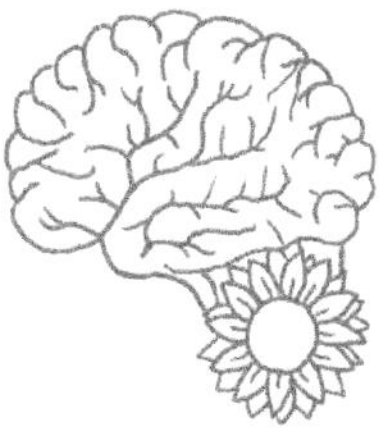

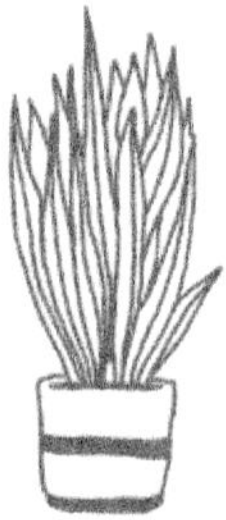

Author's Note

I cannot thank you enough for taking the time to read my poetry collection titled *Short Stay*.
I spent the bulk of my youth hospitalised in adolescent psychiatric hospitals, where I was diagnosed with autism spectrum disorder and paranoid schizophrenia. I struggled with my mental health for many years, and the psychiatric hospital, unfortunately, served as a second home.
Fast forward seven difficult years, I have improved substantially. I am prescribed an antipsychotic medication called clozapine, which has saved my life. I am seeing a wonderful psychiatric nurse. Additionally, I have not been admitted to the psychiatric hospital for a few years now. Because of this, I was able to complete this poetry collection, which was a work-in-progress for several years.
I wrote this poetry collection because I wanted others to understand what it can truly be like when you have a mental illness or when you are hospitalised in a psychiatric hospital. I hope my book raises some awareness about the reality of hospitalisation and losing your mind.
I also hope that my poetry collection serves as comfort, that if you are struggling with your mental health, you are not alone. Mental illness is not a death sentence. *You can and will get better.*
I am proof of that.

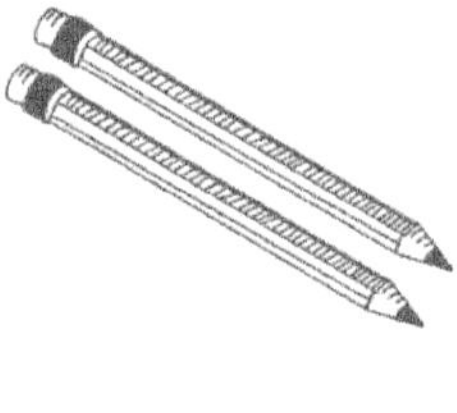

Acknowledgements

I would like to thank my friends and family for supporting me on this journey from the very beginning.
Particularly I would like to express my gratitude to my mother and father. Thank you for staying by my side and being my advocates when I lost my mind. I would also like to thank everyone who visited me in the psychiatric hospital during the most distressing times of my life.
You made those lonely days much more bearable.
Finally, I would like to thank everyone I met while I was hospitalised. The stories you shared with me gave me the inspiration to finally write this poetry collection. I hope that all of you, wherever you may now be, have recovered to some extent, too.

Printed in Great Britain
by Amazon

19487637R00119